Marie Curie

Discoverer of Radium

GREAT MINDS OF SCIENCE

Marie Curie

Discoverer of Radium

Margaret Poynter

Enslow Publishers, Inc.

40 Industrial Road   PO Box 38
Box 398   Aldershot
Berkeley Heights, NJ 07922   Hants GU12 6BP
USA   UK
http://www.enslow.com

Library of Congress Cataloging-In-Publication Data

Poynter, Margaret.
    Marie Curie: discoverer of radium / Margaret Poynter.
        p. cm.
    Includes bibliographical references and index.
    ISBN 0-7660-1875-X (pbk)
    ISBN 0-89490-477-9 (library ed.)
    1. Curie, Marie, 1867-1934—Juvenile literature. 2. Chemists—Poland—Bi-
ography—Juvenile literature. [1. Curie, Marie, 1867–1934. 2. Chemists.
3. Women—Biography.] I. Title.
    QD22.C8P69 1994
    540'.92—dc20
        [B]   93-21224
                                                                 CIP
                                                                  AC

Printed in the United States of America

10 9 8

To Our Readers:
We have done our best to make sure all Internet Addresses in this book were
active and appropriate when we went to press. However, the author and the
publisher have no control over and assume no liability for the material
available on those Internet sites or on other Web sites they may link to. Any
comments or suggestions can be sent by e-mail to Comments@enslow.com
or to the address on the back cover.

Illustration Credits: Archiv Pierre et Marie Curie, pp. 12, 20, 27,
29, 36, 40, 41, 51, 55, 57, 64, 70, 73, 76, 84, 90, 95, 101, 104, 106;
Kim Austin, pp. 10, 32, 46, 48, 81, 108.

Cover Photo Credits: Department of Energy, Atomic Energy Com-
mission (background); Archiv Pierre et Marie Curie (inset).

Contents

Marie's Childhood Years

IN DECEMBER 1903, MARIE CURIE WROTE a letter to her brother. "Dear Joseph," she said, "I thank you most tenderly for your letters. Don't forget to thank Manyusya [Joseph's daughter] for her little letter, so well written, which gave me great pleasure. . . ."

Marie said that she had been sick. Then she said that she and her husband, Pierre, had won half of a Nobel Prize. "With much effort," she wrote, "we have avoided the banquets people want to give in our honor."[1]

The Nobel Prize! What exciting news! Most winners would not have written about anything else. To Marie, though, there was only one good thing about the prize. The money would let Pierre quit one of his teaching jobs. He would get more rest.

Marie did not care about the prize itself. Hundreds of people now wanted to talk to her. They wanted to take her picture. Marie was very timid. She did not like talking to strangers. She did not like people staring at her.[2] And these people were keeping her away from her work. To Marie, work was much more important than fame. She wanted to be left alone in her laboratory.

The laboratory was a leaky shed with a dirt floor. It was here that the Curies discovered radium. The discovery changed science forever, and it gave doctors the way to cure a fatal disease.

❖   ❖   ❖   ❖

Marie Curie was born on November 7, 1867, in Warsaw, Poland. Her father was Vladislav Sklodowski. He was a teacher. Her mother, Bronislawa, was a musician. Marie had three older sisters, Hela, Zosia, and Bronya. She had one brother, Joseph. Everyone called Marie by her nickname, Manya.

At this time, Poland was ruled by Russia. Russian officials had replaced Polish officials. Russian was the official language. Russian books were used in the schools. The Polish people dared not complain. Complainers were put into prison.

When Manya was five, her mother became ill and had to go into a hospital. The family did not have enough money to pay the bills, so they moved to a cheaper apartment. Still there was not enough money. Manya's father took in boarders. The apartment was crowded. It was noisy. But when Manya had a book, nothing bothered her. She had been reading since she was only four.

Manya's mother was in the hospital for one year. Every day, Manya prayed that she would get well. But when she came home, she was still thin and pale. Manya heard her coughing at night. Manya was very worried.

The family kept taking in boarders. One of the boarders had a dreadful disease. Soon, Zosia and Bronya caught it. They shook from chills. They

RUSSIAN

KINGDOM OF
NORWAY
AND SWEDEN

DEN-
MARK

BALTIC
SEA

EMPIRE

BRITISH
ISLES

NETHER-
LANDS

PRUSSIA

• Warsaw

BEL-
GIUM

• Paris

GERMAN
STATES

AUSTRIA-
HUNGARY

FRANCE

SWITZ.

MOLDAVIA

BLACK
SEA

SPAIN

ITALY

OTTOMAN EMPIRE

MEDITERRANEAN SEA

GREECE

c. 1867

*When Marie was born, Poland was part of the Russian Empire.
Many modern European countries do not appear on this map
because they were then part of large empires.*

moaned with fever. Manya prayed for both of them. Bronya recovered, but Zosia died. On a cold January day, nine-year-old Manya went to her sister's funeral. Two years later, her mother died. Manya decided that praying was a waste of time.

The family's luck grew worse. The Russians replaced Polish teachers with Russian teachers. Manya's father had to take a job with much lower pay.

Polish students had a difficult time, also. The teachers gave them lower grades than they gave the Russian students. Sometimes a Russian inspector visited the classrooms. He asked the students questions. All the Polish students were afraid. If they gave a wrong answer, they were called disloyal. One day, the inspector asked Manya some questions. She was very nervous. When the inspector left, she burst into tears.[3]

The Russians caused many problems in school. But Manya's father gave his children lessons at home. He read them books that the Russians had banned. He talked about science and nature. He taught his children to be curious.

Manya studied history and language. She studied mathematics and literature. She wanted to learn everything she could.

Manya was sixteen years old when she graduated. She was happy about the gold medal she received for being the best student in her class. She was not so happy about the books she

Marie (Manya) had three sisters and a brother. From left to right, are Bronya, Joseph, Marie, Hela, and Zosia.

was given. They were Russian books. Manya hated anything that came from that country.

After her graduation, Manya went to the countryside for a vacation. While she was gone, her father's health became poor. He had to stop taking in boarders. Again, the family had to move to a smaller apartment. When Manya returned home, she looked for a job. She wanted to earn some money. Then she could help her father.

But she had a hard time finding a job. The Russians did not want to hire a Polish woman who could read and write. Manya earned a little money by tutoring children. To give the lessons, she walked across town in rain and in snow. She was always on time. But her pupils often made her wait. Many of her pupils were lazy. They would not study. They did not learn their lessons. Some of the parents blamed Manya. They would not pay her for the tutoring.

Manya did not want to be a tutor forever. She wanted to become a scientist. But the Russians would not allow women to go to college. Manya took classes at the "Floating University." This was not a legal school. The students met at night in attics and cellars. If they heard a noise, they trembled. They were afraid of the Russian police. If the students were caught, they would be sent to prison.

To Manya, the Floating University was a dream come true. Here, she read books written in Polish. Here, she learned the true history of Poland. Soon, she was teaching that history to other women. Many of them had never gone to school. She taught them to read and write.

In the Floating University, Manya heard of countries where students were taught the truth. They were not afraid to ask questions. They were not put in prison if they complained. These people would never accept tyranny. They were educated.

Manya had always dreamed of a free Poland.[4] She now knew of a way to help make her dream come true. She continued to educate Polish women. Someday, Manya thought, these women will stop accepting tyranny. They will help to drive the Russians out of Poland.[5]

A Broken Heart

MANYA LIKED THE FLOATING UNIVERSITY. But she had always wanted to go to a real university. So had her sister, Bronya. But there was not enough money for both of them to go. Manya decided that Bronya should be the first to go. After all, Bronya was already twenty. Manya was only seventeen. She could get a job. She could help pay for Bronya's books. When Bronya graduated, Manya could go to school.

Bronya said that Manya was the smarter of the two. Manya should be the first to go.

"No," said Manya. That was the end of the argument.[1]

Bronya went to medical school in Paris, France. Manya became a governess in Warsaw. A few months later, she took a better job in the country. In this family, there were two children at home. One was ten. The other, Bronka, was eighteen, the same age as Manya. The two girls became good friends.

Most people in this part of the country were very poor. Not many of the children went to school. Those who did were taught to read and write Russian, not Polish. Manya wanted to teach these children their country's history and language. She told Bronka her idea. Bronka offered to help. Manya warned her that if they were caught, they might be put in jail.

Bronka paid no attention to her warning. She and Manya put a table and some chairs in Manya's room. Then Bronka told all the neighborhood children to come to the class. The children were poorly dressed. Their hands and faces were dirty. They did not like to sit still. But they watched Manya write letters and words upon a blackboard. They listened as she told them what they were.

They copied them into their notebooks. They came back day after day. Slowly, they learned to read and write Polish.

Manya was happy when her pupils learned their lessons. She wondered when she would be able to return to school? Would it be when Bronya graduates? That will be five years from now. Her father was getting old. By then, he might need her at home.

When would she be able to return to school? Manya's heart ached because the answer might be "never." In a letter to a friend, she wrote that she had no plans for the future.

Most eighteen-year-old girls would not have written such sad words. They would be having too much fun. Manya, however, was not interested in parties or dancing. She did not have any boyfriends. In her spare time, she read books. That Christmas, though, her employers' son, Casimir, came home for the holidays. Casimir was tall and handsome. He fell in love with Manya. And Manya fell in love with him. He and Manya went on picnics. They went for long walks.

Sometimes they just sat and talked. One day Casimir asked Manya to marry him. Manya said yes.

But Casimir's parents would not let him marry Manya. They wanted him to marry a rich girl. Manya had to work for a living. They did not think she was good enough for him.

Now Manya was more unhappy than ever.[2] She could not be with the man she loved. She saw no way that she could go to school. Since she sent half of her salary to Bronya, she could not save any money. She had thought that her employers were her friends. Now she knew they thought of her as just a servant. But she could not quit her job. Her employers paid her well. And Manya needed the money.

Manya did not want her family and friends to worry about her. She tried to keep her letters cheerful. But sometimes she told of her unhappiness. To Joseph, she wrote that she had lost the hope of ever becoming anybody. To a friend, she wrote that she would give half her life to become independent. But later, in a letter to the same friend, she said she was feeling better. She wrote, "First principle: never to let one's self be beaten down by persons or by events."[3]

By 1889, Manya had been a governess for four years. During that time, she had worked very hard and had very little fun. Then her father got a job that paid him a good salary. He could now send money to Bronya. Manya no longer had to send money to her sister. Also, Bronya began to save money to repay Manya. That spring, Manya's employers told her they no longer needed her. In April, she returned to Warsaw. Here, for one year, she worked for another wealthy family.

One day she received a letter from Bronya. Her sister was now a doctor. She was getting married to another doctor. She told Manya to save money for a few months. She could then come to Paris and live with Bronya and her husband. Best of all, she could go to the Sorbonne, a famous French university.

Oh, how Manya wanted to accept the invitation! But what about Joseph and Hela? She had promised them that she would help them go

Monsieur Sklodowski was proud of his daughters, Marie, Bronya, and Hela.

to school. And what about her father? She had promised him that she would live with him. She wanted to make her elderly father happy.

Bronya kept trying to get Manya to come to Paris. In the end, Manya agreed to go live with Bronya in one year's time.

During that year, Manya lived with her father. She earned money by tutoring students. She also entered The Museum of Industry and Agriculture. This "museum" was really a laboratory. Here, Polish students could study science. It was called a museum to fool the Russians.

To Manya, the laboratory was a magical place. At last, she was able to do the work she had always wanted to do. Sometimes at night, she could not sleep. She was too excited about her experiments. When she finally fell asleep, she dreamed about her work. It was always on her mind.

Manya knew there were better laboratories at the Sorbonne. Finally, the day came for her to leave. Soon, she would be studying to become a scientist. She felt as if her real life had finally begun.

Freedom

IT WAS HARD FOR MANYA TO SAY GOOD-BYE to her father. She said she would be gone for only two or three years. Then they would be together always.

Manya's father hugged her. He wished Manya good luck. He told her to work hard.

Three days later, Manya arrived in Paris. To her, it appeared to be a different world. Here, people spoke any language they wanted to speak. They were not afraid to say what they thought. The bookstores were filled with books from all over the world.

Here, there was freedom. Manya had never known freedom before.

On November 3, 1891, Marie enrolled in the Sorbonne. She wrote "Marie Sklodowska" on the papers. (Sklodowska is the feminine form of Sklodowski in Polish.) She was starting a new life. She wanted to use her real name.

In Poland, Marie had not had a good education. Here, most of her classmates were well-educated. Marie had to work very hard to keep up with them. She studied all the time. She was too bashful to say hello to anyone. She did not make many friends. Some of her classmates called her "the mystery woman."

Marie took the omnibus to school every day. It took her one hour to get to school. It took another hour to get home. At night, she tried to study. But Bronya and her husband had many friends. They often came to visit. They talked. They laughed. They played the piano. It was hard for Marie to study. She needed a quiet place. She decided to move close to the school.

All she could afford was a tiny room in an attic.

In the summer, it was very hot. In the winter, it was freezing. During the day, light came through a small hole in the roof. At night, Marie lit an oil lamp. For heat, there was an old coal stove.

Sometimes, Marie did not have enough money to buy coal. To keep warm, she stayed at the library until it closed. Then she went home and studied until two o'clock in the morning. In the winter, her fingers were numb. She shivered. When she went to bed, she kept her clothes on. As she slept, a layer of ice formed on the water in her pitcher.

Marie did not have much money for food. For supper, she often had only bread and tea. Sometimes she was so hungry she became dizzy. Bronya and her husband were worried about her.[1]

Marie would not say that she needed help. She told Bronya she was just working too hard.

One day Marie fainted. Later, Bronya found that she had been eating only cherries and radishes. And she had been sleeping only four hours a night. Bronya made Marie come back to her house. For one week, Marie ate steak and potatoes and thick soup. She then returned to her attic room. There she might be cold and hungry. But there she could study in silence. And to Marie, study was more important than heat or food. It was more important than family or friends.

In July 1893, Marie had to take the test for her degree in physics. Her palms were sweaty. The words on the paper danced before her eyes. Five minutes passed before she could answer the first question. Finally, though, she finished and handed in her paper.

Then came the day when the grades would be announced. Marie could hardly breathe. Suddenly everyone was quiet. The professor was reading the test results. The first name he read was Marie Sklodowska. Marie had not only passed the test. She had earned the highest grade in the class!

Marie was the first woman to receive a degree in physics from the Sorbonne. Physics is the study of natural laws and forces. In 1894, she began working toward a degree in mathematics. She was now twenty-six years old and had no thought of marriage. She had been very hurt by Casimir. And she was too shy to meet other boys.[2] She planned to return to Warsaw and live with her father. In Poland, she could become a teacher. She could try to free her country from the Russians.

One day that spring, Marie went to a friend's house for tea. One of the guests was a famous French scientist. His name was Pierre Curie. He was tall and bearded. He had peaceful eyes. He spoke softly. Marie told Pierre about some work she was doing. Pierre gave her some helpful advice.

Marie liked Pierre. Several times during the next few weeks, the two met at school. They talked about their work. They talked about their families. They took walks in the country. One spring day, Marie said she would soon get her degree in mathematics. She planned to return to Poland. There she would get a job. She would not return to school in the fall.

"Promise me that you will come back," said Pierre. "You have no right to abandon science."

You have no right to abandon *me* is what Pierre

Marie and Pierre enjoyed trips in the country.

really meant. "I believe you are right," Marie said. "I should like to come back very much."[3]

On July 26, 1895, Marie and Pierre were married. The ceremony was simple. There were no wedding rings. There were no big parties. There was no wedding dress. Marie chose a dark blue suit that she could wear to work. For a honeymoon, she and Pierre went on a bicycling trip.

Marie was now busier than ever. She had to study. She was teaching a class. She had to shop and clean house. She had to learn how to cook. Her daughter, Irene, was born in 1897. She was now a wife, a mother, a teacher, and a scientist. She had to handle four jobs at the same time. And then she decided to get a doctorate degree, or Ph.D. in physics.

For this degree, she had to write a long report called a thesis. A thesis must be about new and different research. Marie had read about uranium, a rare metal. Uranium radiates, or gives off, a stream of rays. A lamp gives off light rays.

Marie and Pierre were married in 1895.

The kinds of rays given off by uranium are invisible.

"And where does this radiation get its energy?" asked Pierre. Radiation must have an energy source just as fire is an energy source for heat rays.

"What is the nature of this radiation?" asked Marie.

Metal and wires are electrical conductors. Electricity travels through them as water flows through a pipe. Air is not usually an electrical conductor. But it can conduct electricity when there are ions present. (Ions are small particles.) Uranium rays cause air to become ionized (able to conduct electricity).

How do uranium rays ionize air? Marie wondered.

There were many questions to answer. Marie had found the subject for her thesis.

An Exciting Discovery

WHEN MARIE BEGAN TO STUDY URANIUM, she was already aware of certain facts. One was that all matter is made up of elements. At that time, scientists thought that all the elements had been discovered. Uranium was one of the known elements. Some others included thorium, iron, oxygen, lead, silver, and gold.

Marie knew that each element is composed of a certain type of atom. Atoms are so tiny that it takes billions of them to form a speck of dust. Each atom contains electrons and a nucleus. The nucleus is made up of protons and neutrons. There are many different kinds of atoms. The difference lies

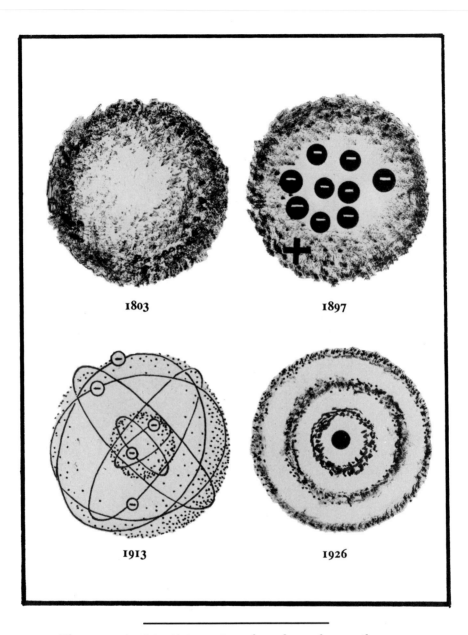

1803   1897

1913   1926

The way scientists picture atoms has changed over the years.
With each new discovery they learned something new about the
atom. The Curies' discoveries have been part of this work.

in the size of the nucleus. The larger the nucleus, the more neutrons and protons it contains.

Marie started her research by collecting many kinds of rocks. These rocks contained many of the known elements. Using extraction methods, she separated the elements from the rocks. Most of the samples she collected were inactive. They did not give off radiation, or energy. Only a few samples gave off radiation. Those samples contained almost pure uranium or thorium.

Now Marie wanted to measure uranium's power to ionize air. She used an electrometer, a device for measuring electric charges. In a small uranium sample, the strength, or intensity, of the radiation was strong. In a large sample, it was much stronger.

Again and again, Marie tested various samples. Some were pure uranium. Some were mixed with another element. Some were solid. Others were powdered. Some were wet, and some were dry. She tested them in strong light and in weak light. Sometimes the uranium was warm.

Sometimes it was cold. But the intensity was always steady and even.

Marie now knew that the radiation did not come from stored-up sunlight or heat. It did not come from anything outside the uranium. She decided it must come from the uranium atom itself. She named the radiation property, or characteristic, radioactivity.

What an exciting, mysterious property, Marie thought. Again and again, she measured the radioactivity of various rocks. Some of them contained only a little uranium or thorium. But they all gave off very strong rays.

One of the rocks Marie used was pitchblende ore. Pitchblende is a dark-colored, rocklike substance with a dull shine. It is made up of small amounts of uranium, oxygen, and a few other elements. But pitchblende is four times more radioactive than pure uranium. Marie was amazed. Where did this strong radiation come from? To her, there was only one answer. Those rocks must contain another radioactive substance. This substance must be a new element. Marie believed that it was. So did Pierre. He left his own work to help Marie.

A new element! Was it possible? What an exciting idea! But it was still only an idea. Marie now had to prove her idea. She had to separate the new element from a uranium sample. Then she could see it. She could weigh it. She could point to it and say, "There it is!"

Pitchblende contains only traces of radioactive material. To obtain just a tiny amount of radioactive material, Marie needed tons of ore. Pitchblende cost a lot of money. How would she pay for it? And what if she obtained the ore? Where could she store it? Where could she do her research?

One of Pierre's friends helped solve the first problem. He knew that uranium salts were used to make dyes. During the process, the uranium was separated from pitchblende. The rest of the pitchblende was thrown away. Pierre's friend helped Marie get the leftover pitchblende. The Curies had to pay for only the shipping.

Marie now needed a space in which to work.

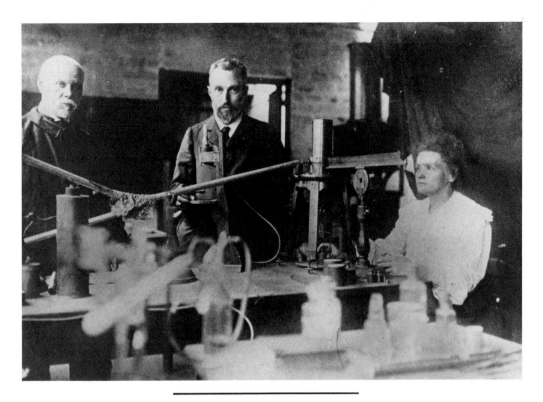

For four years, the shed was the center of the Curies' lives.

In a back courtyard of the school, there was a large shed. It had a leaky roof. It was drafty. It had a dirt floor. The plaster was falling off its walls. It contained only an old stove, some tables, and a blackboard. Someone called it a cross between a stable and a potato cellar.

There was one good thing about the shed. No one else wanted it. Marie did not care about the way it looked. All she wanted was a place to do her work. She could hardly wait for the pitchblende to arrive.

Finally, the great day came. A wagon stopped in front of the shed. The driver threw several heavy cloth bags onto the ground. Marie cut one of them open. She grabbed a handful of the black pitchblende. She ran into the shed. She tested it. The ore was highly radioactive.

The next morning, April 14, 1898, Marie went to work to separate the new element from the other elements. It was a long, slow process. She and Pierre put the pitchblende into a huge cauldron. They ground the pitchblende into powder. They used acid to dissolve the powder. They added certain chemicals that would cause the elements to separate. Then Marie lit a fire under the cauldron. She stirred the poisonous mixture with a long steel rod. Because of the strong fumes, the work was done outside. If it rained, everything had to be moved inside. Even with the windows opened, Marie's eyes and throat stung.

Every day Marie stirred the pitchblende mixture. She lugged jars of it into the shed. Every day, she and Pierre tested the samples. Two months later, she put some of the liquid into a small glass container. She added a chemical. A powdery material separated from the liquid. It sank to the bottom of the container. Marie spooned the powdery material out. She tested it for radiation. It was 150 times more radioactive than an equal amount of pure uranium.

Marie knew that the powder contained the new element. But it was mixed with bismuth, another element. She had to get rid of the bismuth. Pierre put a small amount of the powdery material into a test tube. He heated the tube over a flame. The thick, muddy liquid began to bubble. A black powder formed on the inside of the tube above the liquid. Pierre kept heating the tube until it cracked. He scraped off some of the black powder and tested it. The powder was 330 times more radioactive than an equal amount of uranium. By July, they had a sample that was 400 times more radioactive than uranium.

The Curies knew that the black powder contained a lot of the new element. "You will have to name it," Pierre said to Marie. By this time, Bronya had moved back to Poland. Marie missed her. She missed Poland. For this reason, she named the new element "polonium," after her homeland.[1]

Another discovery helped Marie forget her homesickness. She had removed the polonium from the pitchblende. But the pitchblende was still radioactive. There must be two unknown elements, not just one.

Marie called the second element *radium,* from the Latin word for ray. Radium was even more radioactive than polonium. Marie could hardly wait to see pure radium.

"I wonder what it will be like, what it will look like," she said.

"I don't know," Pierre replied. "I should like it to have a very beautiful color."[2]

Marie continued to work. When Pierre was not teaching his classes, he helped her. The weeks turned into months. The months turned into

Radium was discovered in this old shed.

years. Bit by bit, they treated eight tons of pitchblende. In the summers, Marie suffered from the heat. In the winters, she grew numb from the cold. She fought the dust that mixed itself into her samples. Once she spilled a sample that had taken months to prepare. But as time passed, she had samples that contained more and more radium.

In March 1902, Marie had her first sample of pure radium. It was 900 times more radioactive than uranium. It was silvery-white, like glowing salt. At last, she was able to see it. She was able to weigh it. She had proof that radium existed. Four years had passed since her search had begun.

One night, Marie bathed Irene and put her to bed. Pierre's father, who now lived with them, said good night. Marie and Pierre were relaxing after

To the Curies, the glowing radium was beautiful.

a hard day. Suddenly, Marie stood up. "Suppose we go down there for a moment."

Pierre knew what she meant by "down there." A few minutes later, he was opening the squeaky door of the shed.

"Do you remember when you said to me, 'I should like radium to have a beautiful color?'" Marie asked.

She and Pierre sat in the dark silence. The bluish outlines of the radium glimmered in the darkness. They looked like glowworms. It is more than beautiful, Marie thought. It is magic.[3]

Problems

MARIE HAD A GOOD HUSBAND. SHE HAD A healthy, beautiful daughter. She had proved that radium existed. She should have been completely happy. But there were three problems.

The first was that there was never enough money. She and Pierre had to teach school just to pay rent and buy food. Pierre wanted a good laboratory. They could have discovered radium much sooner in a good laboratory. But all they had was the shed. It seemed they would never have anything better.

The second was the state of their health. Both of them were always tired. The skin on their hands was cracked and raw. Pierre suffered violent pains in his legs. Sometimes he moaned all night. Sometimes he could not get up in the morning. Marie had coughing fits that left her weak and breathless. She was very thin.

The third was that Marie's father had died. Marie wished she had been able to see him one more time. At least, she thought, he knew I had found my radium.[1]

Then one of Bronya's children died. Marie shared her grief. And she worried that something might happen to Irene.

Pierre seemed very sad, too. "It's pretty hard, this life we have chosen," he said one day.

Marie had never heard Pierre complain. She was frightened. Maybe his health was worse than she thought. What if he died?

"We can't exist without each other, can we?" she asked.

"You are wrong," Pierre replied. "Whatever happens, if one has to go on like a body without a soul, one must work just the same."[2]

Marie knew he was right. Day by day, she

continued her research. She wrote papers about her work. Scientists all over the world read those papers. Some of them wanted to study radium. Marie and Pierre sent samples of radium to them.

Marie did not know the energy source of radium's radiation. In one paper, she wrote that it might come from tiny bits of radium being thrown off. Other scientists found that she was partly right. As radium decays, the nucleus of each of its atoms splits into a new atom called radon. At the same time, an alpha particle is given off. This particle creates the heat and light of radiation.

As radon decays, it also gives off an alpha particle and changes into polonium. In the same way, polonium converts to lead. Lead does not change. It is an inactive, or stable, element.

Scientists used to think that all matter was stable. They thought that atoms were unchanging particles. Then Marie and other researchers studied the behavior of radium atoms. It was now evident that atoms have a life of their own. Electrons orbit each atom's nucleus much as the

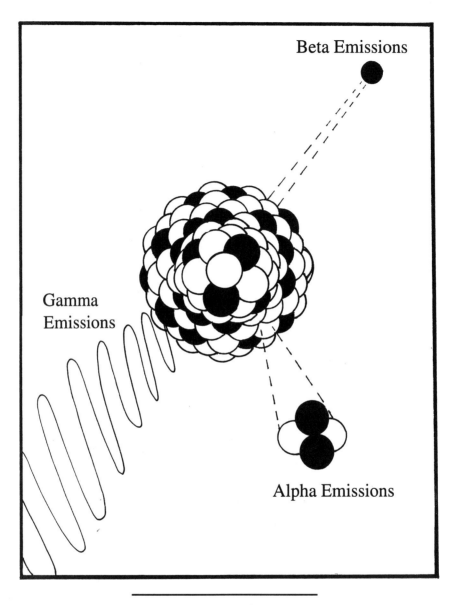

Beta Emissions

Gamma
Emissions

Alpha Emissions

Atoms give off three kinds of radioactive particles: alpha emissions (a neutron), beta emissions (electrons and positrons), and gamma emissions.

earth orbits the sun. Some atoms change into another type of atom, then another. During these activities, there is constant movement.

Later studies showed that radium is two million times more radioactive than uranium. Its rays pass through the hardest materials. Only a thick screen of lead can stop them. Radium gives off heat. Within an hour, it melts its own weight in ice. It colors its glass containers with violet hues. If it is wrapped in paper, it reduces the paper to powder. The light it gives out is enough to read by.

Radium's radiation was found to be contagious. Anything nearby also became radioactive. The dust in the shed was radioactive. Marie and Pierre's clothing was radioactive. The air they breathed was a conductor of radiation.

Pierre knew that radium had changed science forever. One evening he held up a vial of radium. "Here is the light of the future," he said.

Radium also gave doctors a way to treat some kinds of cancer. Marie and Pierre knew that radium causes painful burns. Their hands were

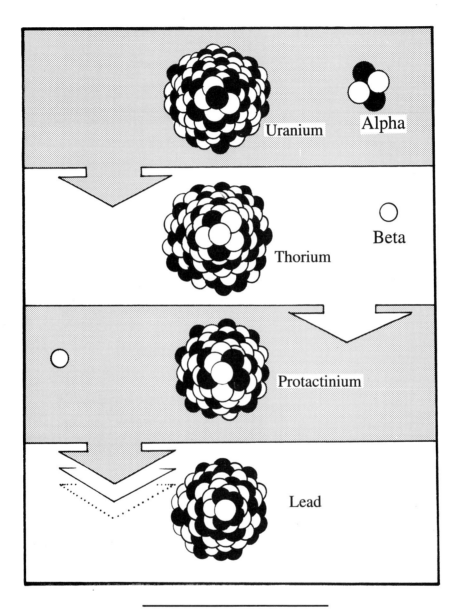

Radioactive, or unstable, elements, change into different elements during radioactive decay. Here, uranium goes through several steps before finally becoming lead, a stable element.

scarred fr   from

new bur   h

burn la

   Pie   ects

living   nto a

ban   n. His

ski   en sore

a   for only

a   r the sore

                        imals with

                       estroyed the

                       s were cured.

                     ncer. With this

                     ved.

   Pierre .   his research. The
news about this miracle   around the world.
Doctors, cancer patients, and scientists needed
radium. Marie and Pierre received a flood of
letters. Hundreds of people wanted a sample. But
in one ton of pitchblende ore, there was less than
an ounce of radium. Radium was worth more than
gold. And only the Curies knew how to produce

it. Marie and Pierre did not think about the money they could make. They wanted to help sick people. They gave their radium away for nothing.

They were also generous with their knowledge. One day they received a letter from some American engineers. The Americans wanted to know how to obtain radium from pitchblende.

Pierre wondered if he and Marie should patent this process. If they did, everyone who used it would have to give them money. They would become rich. They could give Irene everything she needed. They could build a fine laboratory.

But Marie shook her head. "It is impossible," she said. "It would be contrary to the scientific spirit."[3]

Pierre smiled. Marie had given the answer he wanted. He sent the Americans the information they needed.

On June 25, 1903, Marie received her doctor's degree in physics. That same month, she and Pierre went to London to give a lecture on radium. While they were there, they went to a

cr + caw = 14,748,05
id + Racl² = 14,857,3   Racl² = 0,109,25

creuset vide = 10,314,65   Agd = 0,10647
cr + Agd² = 10,421,12

T.39270   Cl = 0.10325   02694
T.02723   0.02630
2.41993   Ra 0.08295   02723

2.91882
2.41993
0.49889

Ra/Cl = 3.154   1.85003
                   0.49889
                   2.34892

Ra = 223.3

AgCl réduit avec Zn et HCl, lavé le creuset, pesé

creuset + argent = 10.3942
                   10.31465
Ag = 0.07955
Cl = 0.02630
d'où AgCl = 0.10564
différence avec AgCl trouvé précédemment
0.00083
y a-t-il eu un peu de Ag non adhérent au creuset?

Every step of an experiment has to be written down. Years after the discovery of radium, Marie's notebooks were still radioactive.

banquet. Pierre wore his everyday coat. Marie wore a plain dark dress. She had no jewelry. Nearby there were women who wore silk gowns. Around their throats, there were diamond necklaces. On their fingers, there were diamond rings. These people were very rich.

Marie and Pierre knew they could have become rich. They could have bought jewels such as these. They could have built many fine laboratories. But they had no regrets. Radium did not belong to them. It belonged to the people who needed it.

A few months later, in November, Marie and Pierre received a telegram. It came from Sweden. They had won half the Nobel Prize in physics! It had been given to them because of their work with radium.

The lives of the Curies were soon to be changed forever.

6

A Tragedy

THE NOBEL PRIZES ARE GIVEN OUT IN Stockholm, Sweden. A French official accepted the Curies' award for them. Neither Marie nor Pierre was feeling well. They could not make the long train trip. Besides, they had too much to do in Paris. They had discovered radium. But their work was not done. It had just begun. Marie did not want to give speeches. She did not want to be with strangers. She just wanted to be with her family. She just wanted to work.

No one seemed to care what Marie wanted. She received hundreds of letters and telegrams. Newspaper people followed her and Pierre. They were asked to go to meetings. Banquets were given in their honor. Everywhere they went, men and women crowded around them. They all wanted to see a famous woman scientist. They wanted to talk to her, to touch her. They wanted to see the inside of the shed. They wanted to see Irene. They even wanted to see the family cat. There was no peace at home or at work.

Marie had always been timid. All the attention frightened her. "One would like to dig into the ground somewhere to find a little peace," she wrote to Joseph. "Our life has been altogether spoiled by honors and fame."[1]

Marie had to get away for a few days. She and Pierre went to the beach. They stayed at a fisherman's cottage. One day Marie was sitting on the front steps. She was shaking the sand from her shoes. A stranger walked up to her. He was a reporter. He wanted to know how she felt about her work. He asked her about her family. He asked about her childhood.

Marie turned her head away. "In science," she said, "we must be interested in things, not in persons."[2]

The shed became crowded with equipment and radium samples.

One good thing came with the Nobel Prize. Marie and Pierre received a large amount of money. Marie shared that money with many other people. One of them was Bronya. Another was a poor woman who had given her free French lessons. A third was a young man who had worked in their laboratory. She sent gifts to other members of her family. She helped poor Polish students.

Pierre was now able to quit one of his teaching jobs. The Curies also hired a laboratory helper. Marie hoped that Pierre could get more rest. Perhaps his health would improve.

That wish was not granted. Pierre continued to have vicious attacks of pain. Sometimes he was so weak he could barely walk. Marie was very worried about him. She herself was always tired. For twenty years, she had worked without stopping. She had never had time to enjoy her family. Suddenly she wished she could stop being a famous woman. She wished she could just rest. She wished people would leave her alone. She wished she had never heard of radium.

At this time, she was expecting her second child. Not even that good news cheered Marie up. She did not think she should have another baby. She said that life was too hard, even for children.

Marie's daughter, Eve, was born in December 1904. The birth left Marie feeling even more tired. She did nothing but sleep. As weeks passed,

Marie was grateful that Eve and Irene were healthy.

though, she began to feel better. A visit from Bronya helped. So did the smiles and gurgles of her newborn child. She started teaching her classes again.

She also returned to her research. Now, however, she was able to work in a proper place. The Sorbonne let the Curies share a laboratory on the school grounds. The school also gave Marie a salary. Once again, she looked forward to going to work.

The Curies were sad when they moved out of the shed. They had come to love its wet walls and rotten planks.

On Easter weekend in 1906, the Paris weather was good. Marie and Pierre decided to go to the country for a few days. On Easter Sunday, they and the children went to the woods. Irene chased butterflies. Fourteen-month-old Eve rode on Pierre's shoulders.

The next day, Marie and Pierre watched Eve and Irene romp on the grass. Pierre turned to Marie and touched her hair. "Life has been sweet with you," he murmured.[3] That afternoon, the family picked flowers. Later, Pierre went back to Paris. Marie and the children followed on Wednesday.

The weather had changed. It was cold. A sharp wind was blowing. The rain beat on the windows. The streets were slippery.

On Thursday, April 19, it was still raining. The skies were dark. That morning, Marie was busy with the children. Pierre called good-bye to her. Marie heard the front door slam. Pierre left in a hurry.

Marie had several errands to do that day. She told Pierre's father that she would be home at noon. But she was delayed. She did not return until six o'clock that evening. Two of Pierre's friends were waiting for her. Marie looked at them. She looked at Pierre's father.

"Pierre was run over by a cart," one of the friends said. "He is dead." He went on to tell about the accident. Pierre had not been looking where he was going. The driver of the horse-drawn wagon yelled at him. He could not stop in time.

Pierre tried to get out of the way. But the rear wheels ran over him.

There was a long silence. Marie did not move. She did not cry out. Finally, in a low voice, she murmured, "Pierre is dead? Dead? Absolutely dead?"[4]

"Yes," Pierre's father replied. He reached out his arms to Marie.

Marie did not move. She looked at the flowers they had picked in the country. They were still fresh. She went into the garden. It had stopped raining. The trees were dripping on her. She sat on a wet bench. She bowed her head and covered her face with her hands.

Pierre's death seemed to take the life from Marie. Her family tried to console her. Pierre's family and all their friends tried to comfort her. She would not listen when they spoke. She would not answer them. She moved swiftly. She did not seem to notice anyone or anything. Her blank stare frightened Bronya.

Meanwhile, there were questions to be answered. Who would continue Pierre's research at the Sorbonne? Who would take charge of his laboratory? Who would teach his classes? Marie did not seem to care. But Bronya and Jacques, Pierre's brother, talked to the school officials. They said that Marie should carry on Pierre's work. She should teach his classes. She should be put in charge of the laboratory.

But Marie is a woman, said the officials. No woman has ever been given such work. Bronya and Jacques said that Marie should have the job. No one else would be able to do it. Finally, the officials agreed.

Marie had been offered a pension by the government. She refused it. "I am young enough to support myself and my children," she said. But should she take over Pierre's jobs? Marie was not sure. She talked to Pierre's father. He told her she should take them.

Marie thought for a minute. She remembered Pierre's words. "Whatever happens . . . one must work."

She sighed and straightened her shoulders. "I will try," she said.

It was a Monday afternoon the following November when Marie entered a crowded lecture hall at the Sorbonne. Her face was pale. She stared straight ahead. There was a storm of applause. Marie nodded. The audience quieted down. Marie began to speak.

"When one considers the progress that has been made in physics in the past ten years, one is surprised at the advance that has taken place in our ideas concerning electricity and matter. . . ."[5]

The students were astounded. Professor Pierre Curie had ended his last lecture with that sentence. Professor Marie Curie was starting where he had left off.

Life Without Pierre

MARIE'S DAYS HAD ALWAYS BEEN BUSY. Now she had to teach Pierre's classes. She had to do their research alone. She had to raise Eve and Irene without him. She was glad that Pierre's father lived with her. He loved the children, and they loved him.

Early every day, Marie boarded the train to the Sorbonne. All morning, she taught classes. For lunch, she nibbled at bread or fruit as she walked to the laboratory. It was late in the afternoon when she took the train home.

Keeping busy did not help her recover from Pierre's death. But she never let anyone see her

After Pierre's death, Marie had to raise Eve and Irene by herself.

cry. She would not let anyone comfort her. She refused to talk about her nightmares. She never mentioned her despair. But her family and friends saw her staring into space. They saw her rub her scarred fingers against each other. They saw the tired lines in her pale face.

In a diary, Marie poured out her feelings to Pierre. "I want to tell you that I no longer love the sun or the flowers. The sight of them makes me suffer."

"Everything is over," she wrote. "Everything, everything, everything. I went to the laboratory. . . . I tried to make a measurement. . . . But I felt the impossibility of going on."[1]

She told a friend that even her children failed to make her happy. Still, she tried to be a good mother. She and her daughters took long walks. They took trips on bicycles. They went swimming. The girls worked in the garden. They learned to cook and to sew. They took music lessons.

Marie told Eve and Irene that they must be able to earn a living when they grew up. She taught them arithmetic.

"You must get so you never make a mistake," she told them. "The secret is in not going too fast."

She taught science to her daughters and their friends. She was upset when she saw a messy laboratory table. "Don't tell me you will clean it up afterward! One must never dirty a table during an experiment."[2]

One day Marie held up a jar of hot liquid. She asked her students to tell her the best way to keep the liquid hot. The young people discussed various methods. Finally, Marie smiled and put a lid on the jar. She had taught the students that the simplest way is often the best way.

Professor. Researcher. Laboratory director. Mother. Marie worked hard at each job. She also wrote two science books. She became even more famous. She was given honors and awards. In 1911, she won the Nobel Prize in chemistry. No one else had ever won two Nobel Prizes.

Not everyone admired and loved Marie Curie. Many were jealous of her fame. There were some French people who called her "that foreign woman." They made up stories about her. "She does not deserve to be honored," they said. "A woman should not be doing a man's work. Why doesn't she go to church? Why doesn't she want to talk to reporters? Why does she hide from people? She must be a bad person."

"Why does Madame Curie have so many men friends?" they asked each other. "She should have only women friends." No one asked Marie. She would have said that most of her friends were scientists. And most scientists were men.

Pierre's father died in 1910. At that time, Marie still had not recovered from Pierre's death. She could not even say "my husband" or "your father." The gossip added to her sadness. She hated fame more than ever.

Marie had never eaten well. She had never rested enough. She was often thin and sickly. Now, her health grew worse. Joseph, Hela, Jacques, and Bronya came to Paris to be with her. Marie remained unhappy and unwell.

By December 1912, she appeared to be dying. She was taken to a nursing home. Here, she regained some of her strength. But then she needed an operation. When she returned to Paris, she was thin and weak. Sometimes, she could barely stand up. She wondered what the future held for her.

Slowly she regained her strength. And then she received some good news. Russia was losing its hold on Poland. The Polish people had more freedom. Some Polish scientists wanted to build a radioactivity laboratory in Warsaw. They asked Marie to be its director.

Marie wanted to take the offer. To her, Paris had become an unfriendly place. It held many bad memories.

One thing held her back. The Curies had always dreamed of working in a fine laboratory. Now the French government was building the French Radium Institute. Pierre would have wanted Marie to become one of its directors. She decided to stay in Paris.

Marie helped plan the French Radium Institute. She said it should have large rooms and big windows. She planted rose bushes in the garden. As she patted down the earth, she felt peaceful. She had not felt that way since Pierre's death. For the first time in months, she smiled. She still missed Pierre. But she knew her own life was not yet over.

One day she heard that the shed was going to be destroyed. Marie rushed to see it for the last time. Pierre's handwriting was still on the blackboard. Marie stood quietly for a few minutes. It seemed to her that the door might open. Pierre would enter the shed. Their research could continue. Their life together could go on.

Marie shook her head. She had work to do. She turned and left the shed for the last time.

Early in 1913, Marie went to Warsaw for the opening of the radioactivity laboratory. For the first time, she gave a lecture in Polish. Polish citizens packed the hall. Everywhere she went, her fellow Poles welcomed her. A feeling of freedom filled the air.

Over the next few months, Marie grew stronger. That summer she and her daughters hiked through the Alps. The group included the

Marie and Albert Einstein enjoyed sharing ideas.

famous scientist Albert Einstein. Einstein liked to talk to Marie. One day, the hikers were climbing up a steep rock. Einstein was deep in thought. He barely noticed the deep crevasse beside him. Suddenly, he stopped and grabbed Marie's arm. "You understand," he said, "what I need to know is exactly what happens to the passengers in an elevator when it falls into emptiness."[3]

Everyone except Marie laughed. To her, the statement did not sound silly. She alone understood that he was serious. He was thinking about gravity. As with Marie, Einstein's work was always on his mind.

A World at War

IN JULY 1914, MARIE'S LABORATORY IN the French Radium Institute was finished. Carved above the door were these words: *Institut du Radium, Pavillon Curie* (in English, The Institute of Radium, Curie Pavilion).

These buildings "are the temples of the future," Marie said. "It is there that humanity grows bigger, strengthens and betters itself."[1]

The institute was ready for its workers and its director. And Marie was anxious to start her new job. But first, she wanted to take a short vacation. Irene and Eve and their governess had already

The Paris Radium Institute was one of Marie's dreams come true.

gone to a beach cottage. Marie was to join them on August 3.

But war was breaking out in Europe. On August 1, Marie wrote to her daughters. She told them that things seemed to be getting worse. She did not know if she could leave Paris.

The next day, the Germans invaded France. They had already occupied Poland. Marie was worried about her family. She could not think about her research. She could think only about helping France. She stopped teaching her classes. Now she could give all of her time to war work. How can I help the most? she wondered. By giving X-ray equipment to hospitals, she decided. X rays could help doctors "see" inside wounded soldiers' bodies. They would know exactly where there was a bullet. They would know where a shell fragment was hidden.

Many X-ray machines were needed. Marie collected the machines from the school. She collected them from her own laboratory. She collected them from the people who made the machines. All these machines were given to nearby hospitals.

But what about the patients in base hospitals? What about the soldiers on the front lines? Marie turned an ordinary car into a mobile X-ray unit. It could follow the army as it moved from place to place. Marie was often seen turning the crank to start the car. She changed her own tires. She cleaned her own dirty carburetor. She did not like to depend on anyone else.

The Germans started marching toward Paris. Marie could have gone to be with Irene and Eve. She decided to stay where she was. In Paris, she could help in the war effort. And she did not want to leave her new laboratory. If I am there, she thought, the Germans may not plunder it.

Marie was not afraid of the Germans. But she was worried about the gram of radium in the laboratory. It would be safer in another city. She carried the radium in a lead case. The other train passengers did not know who she was. They did not know what was inside her case. Only Marie

During World War I, Marie turned cars into mobile X-ray units.

knew that what she carried was worth one million francs.

By the next afternoon, the radium was inside a bank vault. Marie went back to Paris. She wanted to protect her laboratory. She was eager to help win the war. But a friend saw how tired she was. He made her lie down.

The German army was stopped before it reached Paris. It was now safe for Irene and Eve to come home. Meanwhile, Marie had talked twenty rich women into giving her their cars. She turned them into mobile X-ray units. She talked officials into giving her supplies. Some of them argued with her.

"Civilians must not bother us," they said. Marie forgot that she was timid. She nagged until she got what she needed.

Marie kept one of the mobile units for her own use. She was always prepared to answer a call for help. As soon as she hung up the telephone, she ran to her car. She sped toward the front lines.

Sometimes a sentry stopped her. "What's a woman doing out here?" they demanded. Marie showed them her papers. The sentry then sent her on her way. In a Belgian hospital, many people did not know who Marie was. They thought she was a nurse's helper. Marie did not mind. She did not say that she knew the king and queen of Belgium.

The base hospital was often nothing but a bombed-out building. Marie quickly set up her equipment. One after another, wounded soldiers were X-rayed. Most of them did not know what an X ray was. "Will it hurt?" they asked.

"Not any more than having your picture taken," Marie replied. A few words put the men at ease.

Sometimes there were a hundred soldiers waiting. Marie was often in the darkroom developing X rays for days. She ate when she had a minute. She slept anywhere.

One day she was returning to Paris. Her driver twisted the steering wheel too hard. The car landed upside down in a ditch. Marie was buried under several heavy cases. Her driver ran around outside the car. "Madame! Madame! Are you dead?" he cried.

Marie laughed. "No," she said. She was not worried about her bruises. She was worried that her X-ray machine was broken.

Marie visited over 300 hospitals during the war. She later gave 200 of them their own X-ray machines. They would no longer have to call on her for help.

By 1915, Irene and Marie had become more than mother and daughter. They had become partners. Irene had taken a course in radiology, the study of X rays. She could now go to the hospitals in Marie's place. Marie was busy moving into her new laboratory. She brought the gram of radium back to Paris.

Marie never thought of the radium as hers. She said it belonged to France. It was used as an "emanation service." The gas the radium gave off was put into tubes. The tubes were sent to hospitals. This emanation was used to cure bad scars and skin lesions.

Marie could not find enough trained

radiologists. She and Irene started a course in radiology. From 1916 to 1918, they trained 150 men and women. Some of them were not well-educated. One of them had been a chambermaid. Marie helped her get a better job.

Later, twenty United States soldiers came to Marie's laboratory. There they got their first instruction in radioactivity.

Marie faced hardships and dangers during the war. But she never spoke of them. She never spoke of her worry about her family in Poland. She did not speak of her memories of badly wounded soldiers. But she could not forget their groans and shrieks.

One day, Marie was working in her laboratory. The sound of gunfire startled her. She asked an assistant what was happening. "The war is over!" was the reply. Trembling with joy, Marie rushed outside. She spent the rest of the morning watching the cheering men and women who crowded the streets. They were all happy that France was out of danger. Marie was even happier because Poland was set free at last. She thought

*After World War I, many of Europe's borders changed. Poland
became an independent nation.*

of the students in the Floating University. She thought of the poor women she had taught to read and write. They and thousands of other people had made her dream come true.

Later, Marie wrote to her brother, Joseph. "We did not hope to live this moment ourselves. We thought it might not even be given to our children to see it—and it is here!"[2]

As she wrote those words, Marie was already busy planning the future. Now that the war was over, she could return to her laboratory and the work she loved.

A Trip to the United States

THE WAR DISRUPTED MARIE'S RESEARCH. It left her tired and ill. It left her almost poor. She had given all her money to help France. She wanted supplies for her laboratory. But she was not able to buy them.

But now Marie was able to spend time with Irene and Eve. The three of them skated, hiked, and rode horses. Marie was excited about working with Irene in the laboratory. She rejoiced to see Eve studying music. She was getting over Pierre's death. She was able to get more rest. Slowly her health improved.

But she had problems with her ears. They

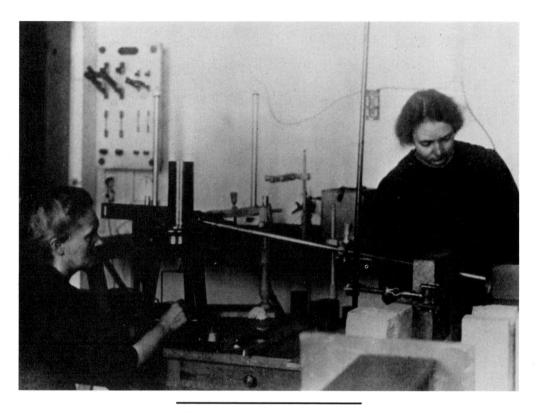

Marie and Irene became partners in the laboratory.

buzzed all the time. Her eyes bothered her, too.
She had trouble going up and down stairs. At
times, she needed help crossing a street. She
could read only big letters. Some operations
helped her see better. She did not want anyone to
know about this problem. Her eye doctor did not
know her real name. She told him she was
"Madame Carre."

Can radium cause eye and ear problems? Marie wondered.[1] More and more, she believed it did. She had not protected herself from its rays. Now she had health problems. One scientist had spilled some strong radioactive material on herself. She died a short time later. Another scientist had a polonium tube explode in her face. She lost her hair. She also had stomach problems. Other people who had worked with radium had sharp leg pains. Pierre had suffered from such pains.

Marie taught her students to protect themselves from radioactivity. Lead screens stopped the rays. Laboratory coats were changed often. The laboratory had plenty of fresh air. The students did not touch the tubes of radium with bare hands. They had regular blood tests.

Marie herself often did not follow the safety rules. After all, she said, she had worked with radium for many years. And she was still getting around very well.

Marie still did not like to talk to reporters. When she did, she would talk only about science.

She would not talk about her personal life. One day an American reporter, Missy Meloney, asked to see Marie. Marie said no. But Missy was as stubborn as Marie. She asked again and again. Finally Marie said yes.

On a day in May 1920, Missy entered Marie's office. Marie saw that Missy was nervous. To put her at ease, Marie talked about America.

"America has about fifty grams of radium," she said. She told Missy that her laboratory had only one gram.

"If you had the whole world to choose from, what would you take?" Missy asked.

"I need a gram of radium to continue my research," Marie said. "But I cannot buy it."[2]

Later Missy found that a gram of radium cost $100,000. She went back to the United States. She asked American women to help buy radium for Marie. Money came from all over the country. It came from rich women. It came from poor women. It came from college students. In less than a year, Missy had collected over $100,000.

"The money has been found," she wrote to Marie. "The radium is yours."

There was one problem. Many of the women who had given money wanted to see Marie. She had to go to the United States to get the radium.

Marie had always fled from crowds. The idea of a visit to the United States terrified her. She said she could not go.

But Missy would not take no for an answer. She calmed all of Marie's fears. Besides, Eve and Irene were eager to take the trip. Right away, they started to pack. They bought Marie four new dresses. Marie thought they were wasting money. She liked her old, faded clothes.

Four weeks later, they boarded the *SS Olympic*. On the ship, there was a closet in Marie's cabin. When the door was opened, a light went on. Marie went inside the closet. She shut the door. The light went out. But Marie could not find a switch. Soon it was time for dinner. Marie was still inside the closet. She was trying to see how the light worked.

At New York harbor, a big crowd greeted the

ship. There were troops of Girl Scouts. Hundreds of Polish women waved red and white roses. American, French, and Polish flags waved in the breeze. People were taking Marie's picture.

"Look this way, [Madame] Curie!" they shouted. "Turn your head to the left! Lift your head! Look this way! This way! This way!"[3] Everyone wanted to see "The Radium Woman." Marie had not yet left the ship. But she was already frightened.

During the next few weeks, newspapers shouted about Marie's visit.

"SIMPLE CHARM OF TIRED VISITOR," read one headline.

"JUST TIMID LITTLE WOMAN," read another.

"PLAINLY DRESSED SCIENTIST," read a third.

Marie went to dinners for 500 people. She went on long trips in a car. She made her way through mobs of people. Tearful men and women tried to kiss her hands. They tried to touch her dress. They applauded when she spoke.

There were visits to women's colleges. Students waved flags and flowers. Hundreds of them ran to meet Marie's car. Marie was stunned by the noise. She was afraid of being crushed. She did not like being stared at. Even at the Grand Canyon, people stared at her.

In France, Marie was always able to hide from people. In the United States, she could not hide. Irene and Eve now saw how everyone loved their mother. They also saw how timid she was. They acted as Marie's "bodyguards." One of them was always by her side.

On May 20, 1921, Marie visited the White House in Washington, D.C. President Warren G. Harding called Marie a "noble creature," a "devoted wife and loving mother." He spoke of her years of "crushing toil." He then passed a silken cord over her head. On that cord was the key to her container of radium.

The trip to the United States taught Marie something. As a student, she could hide in an attic. As a researcher, she could hide in her laboratory. But she was now a famous woman. As

President Harding praised Marie for her work.

a famous woman, she had wanted a gram of radium. And she had received it.

There were other things Marie wanted. She wanted countries to share their scientific ideas. She wanted peace in the world. She wanted to help poor students go to college.

Marie was happy that Warsaw had a radioactivity laboratory. But she also wanted that city to have a radium institute, where cancer patients could be treated.

There was only one way to get everything Marie wanted. She had to meet people. She had to talk to people. She had to answer their questions.

Marie had once said, "In science, we must be interested in things, not in persons." She now knew better.[4] Someone had to tell people about those "things." She was going to have to be that someone. She had to forget that she was timid. She had to overcome her fears.

At the age of fifty-five, Marie had to come out of hiding.

An Ordinary Day

FOR MARIE, THE TRIP TO THE UNITED States was just a beginning. Suddenly she was a world traveler. She went to Brazil and to Spain. She went to Italy, the Netherlands, England, and Switzerland. She met kings and queens and presidents. She visited laboratories and universities. She spoke at meetings and in classrooms. Her face and name were known all over the world. Her picture was even hung in a temple in China.

Marie went to Poland four times. She was not there just to see her family. She wanted to raise money for a radium institute. With Bronya's help, she flooded the country with posters. "Buy a brick for the Marie Sklodowska Institute," the posters said. Brick by brick, the walls were raised. A few years later, the building was finished.

But the institute had no radium. Without it, cancer could not be treated. Missy Meloney started collecting money again. Soon the institute had its radium.

Again Marie went to the United States. She met with crowds of people. Henry Ford gave her a car. And President Herbert Hoover invited her to the White House. She stayed there overnight. Usually, only important foreign officials spent the night at the White House.

During her travels, one thing bothered Marie. "When they talk to me about my 'splendid' work," she said, "it seems to me that I am already dead. . . . It seems to me that the services I might still render don't mean much to them."[1]

Despite her fame, Marie did not change. She carried the same old brown handbag. She wore the same plain black dresses. Her work was still more important than any praise. She was still timid. When she was with strangers, her throat was dry. Her hands were cold. She seldom smiled or laughed. She always felt alone, even when she was with other people.

Honors meant nothing to Marie. When she arrived home, she put her medals away. But she kept out the banquet menus she had collected. They were made of heavy cardboard. She scribbled notes on the backs of them.

In 1926, Irene had married Frederic Joliot. Frederic worked in the French Radium Institute. Now Marie had two helpers instead of one. Irene and her husband shared her worries. They talked about her research. They gave her new ideas. At home, Eve became Marie's closest companion. Eve was a musician. Marie enjoyed hearing her play the piano.

Marie arrived at the institute at nine o'clock every morning. There were always students waiting at the door. Some asked questions. Some wanted advice. Some wanted to talk about their research results. Marie knew all about each student's work. She answered any question. With her help, each problem was solved. She and a

At the Paris Radium Institute, Marie continued her research.

student often met in the garden. As they talked, Marie did not notice the bad weather. Someone would have to remind her to go inside.

Marie was very busy. But she always found time for her students. They were like her family. When she was with them, she smiled a lot. Sometimes she even laughed. But there were some sad times, too. One of her favorite pupils drowned in a river.

"I am quite overcome," she wrote. "His mother said he had passed the best years of his life in the laboratory. What was the good of it, if it had to end like this?"

Marie spent part of the day doing her own work. Sometimes her research did not go well. Then she slumped into a chair. She crossed her arms. She gazed into space. She felt old. Once someone asked her what was wrong.

"That polonium has a grudge against me," she muttered.[2]

More often, her work went well. Then she went into the garden. She touched the flowers. She smiled up at the sky. She felt young. Marie's happiness depended on her work.[3]

All day long people came to Marie's office. Students needed her help. Reporters wanted to ask questions. Other scientists wanted to exchange ideas. Marie often forgot to eat lunch. Then someone would put bread and fruit beside her.

Every day Marie received dozens of letters. Some were from cancer patients. They thanked her for discovering radium. Some of these people did not know Marie's address. On the envelope, they wrote only "Mme. Curie, Paris" or "Mme. Curie, scientist, France." Every mailman knew where Marie Curie lived and worked. The letters were always delivered.

The laboratory was often short of supplies. Marie had to visit various officials. She begged. She pleaded. She demanded. Some officials called her a nag. But they gave her what she needed.

Twice a week, at five o'clock, she lectured to classes. She was always nervous on those days. She had taught classes for twenty-five years. But she never overcame her stage fright.

In Marie's spare moments, she wrote articles. She also wrote a book about Pierre's life.

At eight or nine o'clock, Marie went home. She and Eve ate dinner together. Marie told Eve about her work at the laboratory. Eve told Marie the news of the world. They talked about the poor people in France. They needed better houses. They needed better schools. Marie was especially worried about poor women and young girls. She wanted each of them to have a good family life and some work that interested them.

Marie still missed Pierre. But she never spoke about her grief. She seldom mentioned her own poor health. She did talk about how much she missed Hela and Bronya and Joseph. She did not like growing old without them.

After dinner, Marie went to her study. She did not use her desk. She sat on the floor. There she had room to spread out her books and papers. As she worked, she talked to herself in Polish. At two or three o'clock, she stood up.

"Ah, how tired I am," she said.[4] And then she went to bed.

The End

EVE AND IRENE TRIED TO GET MARIE TO slow down. "You've worked hard all your life," they said. "Now you should rest."

But Marie could not take the time to rest. She was teaching classes. She was building a factory for the treatment of ores. She was writing a book.

And she could not stop her research. Her laboratory was her life. The buzzing in her ears, her illnesses, her constant fever, her dizziness, her poor eyesight—nothing could keep her from her work.

Marie tried to prove that she was healthy. She went skating and skiing. She went on long walks.

She rode a bicycle. Bronya came to visit in the spring of 1934. On the Easter holiday, she and Marie went on a long trip. Marie was tired, and the weather was very cold. The vacation house was icy. Marie became chilled. She shivered in Bronya's arms. She was afraid that she would not be able to finish her book.

The next day, the weather was warm. Marie felt much better. For the next few days, she rested. Then she and Bronya went back to Paris. Bronya was still worried about Marie. She wanted her to see a doctor. But Marie said she was all right. The sisters hugged each other. They said good-bye. Bronya waved to Marie from the train.

After Bronya left, Marie had good days and bad days. On the bad days, she stayed home and worked on her book. On the good days, she went to the laboratory. She was always tired and weak. One day she had chills and fever. Eve called a doctor. He told her to stay in bed.

Marie did not follow his order. Her fever was so high she had to go home. "Wait for me a little

To Marie, her laboratory was her life.

while," she told a group of her students. "I am going off to rest for a few days."[1]

Before she left, she walked through the laboratory garden. She told the gardener to take care of a sickly looking rose vine. Then she drove away in her car.

Marie went to bed as soon as she got home. Eve told her she had to see a doctor. Marie felt so sick she did not argue. The doctor found that her lungs were inflamed. He said she should go to a hospital in the mountains. The doctor said the clear air would make Marie feel better.

As they prepared to make the trip, Marie talked to Eve about her research. She talked about the institute in Warsaw. She spoke of Eve's future. She said she hoped that Irene would win the Nobel Prize.

She also talked to her helper at the laboratory. "I count on you to put everything in order," she said. "We shall resume this work after my holiday."[2] As she talked, Marie grew weaker and weaker.

Eve did not want her mother to go to the

mountains. She said the trip was too long. But four more doctors looked at Marie. They all said the mountain air would help her. Marie should leave right away, they urged.

The trip was very hard on Marie. She had a high fever. She ached all over. When she arrived at the hospital, she fainted. Eve knew her mother might be dying. But she would not allow any treatment that would be painful. She wrote to Missy that Marie was very sick. "She is suffering so much I cannot bear to look at her. I have to go out of the room to cry."

For several days, Marie barely spoke. Then her mind started to wander. "I can't express myself properly," she said. "My head's turning." "Was it made with radium or mesothorium?" "I'm trembling so."

When the doctor tried to give her a shot, she said she did not want it.

"I want to be left in peace," she said.[3]

Those were her last words. At dawn, Marie's heart stopped beating. Her scarred hands were finally still. It was July 4, 1934. Marie Curie was

Marie died a short while after this picture was taken.

sixty-six years old. She had died of leukemia. The disease had been caused by radiation.

The news of Marie's death spread around the world. Hela was in Warsaw when she heard about it. Joseph was on a train. He had been rushing to see Marie. Bronya also was hurrying to France. Marie's many friends were stunned by the news. Her students sobbed.

"We have lost everything," one of them wrote.

Missy Meloney was one of Marie's best friends. Eve sent Marie's watch to Missy. The watch had once belonged to Pierre. "It has no value," she wrote, "except that she wore it always and liked it. It was on her table near her bed when she died."

Marie was buried above Pierre. Irene and Joseph threw a handful of Polish soil into her grave.

One year later, Marie's book was published. Its title consisted of only one bold word: *Radioactivity*. It was Marie Curie's last message to her young "lovers of physics."

Marie Curie became a role model for many young scientists who followed in her footsteps.

The Building Blocks of Science

IN 1895, WILHELM ROENTGEN DISCOVERED X rays. These rays go through wood, cloth, and flesh. They do not go through thick lead and bone.

A few months later, Antoine Becquerel found that uranium gives off rays. These rays go through paper and glass. He shared the 1903 Nobel Prize in physics with Marie and Pierre Curie.

Marie Curie read about the work of these two men. What she learned helped her with her own work. Marie's discoveries helped other scientists. Building block upon building block, scientific knowledge grows. Marie's work helped form our

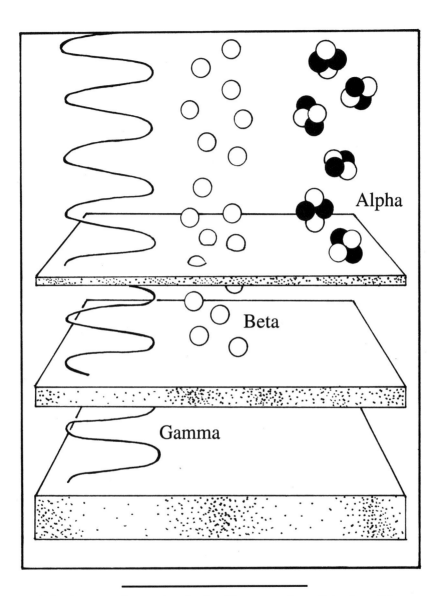

Alpha

Beta

Gamma

Scientists now know that lead will protect them from harmful radiation. Alpha particles can be blocked by paper and beta particles can be blocked by brass, but only lead will stop gamma rays.

modern world. We now have atomic power. We have atomic submarines. We have radiation treatments for cancer. Radioactive dating reveals the ages of rocks and fossils. Radiation finds cracks in machinery and in airplane parts. It measures the thickness of metal pipes. It preserves and sterilizes food.

Understanding radioactivity helps us understand how our sun works. Understanding our sun helps us understand our solar system. It helps us understand our whole universe.

Marie Curie died in 1934, but her work will keep her memory alive forever.

ACTIVITIES

Making a Thermometer

Marie Curie showed her students how to make a thermometer. Now you can make a thermometer. See how substances expand, or grow larger, when they are heated. See how substances contract, or grow smaller, when they are cooled.

Materials:

- a small soda bottle
- modeling clay
- a clear plastic drinking straw
- food coloring
- an index card

Procedure:

1. Fill the bottle about four-fifths full of water. Add some food coloring.

2. Dry the lip of the bottle. Squeeze some clay around the rim. Put the straw halfway into the bottle. Press the clay around the straw. Make a tight seal.

3. Tape the card to the straw. At room temperature, note the height of the water in the straw. Mark the height on the card.

4. Place the bottle in a sunny spot for one hour. Note the height of the water in the straw. Mark the height on the card.

5. Place the bottle in a shallow pan filled with ice water. Note the height of the water in the bottle. Mark the height on the card.

Measuring Heat Rays

The sun gives off heat rays. So does fire. Heat rays radiate outward in straight lines and in all directions. In this experiment, you can measure heat rays.

Materials:

- a 100-watt light bulb
- a thermometer
- a piece of cardboard
- a pencil
- a sheet of paper

Procedure:

1. Switch the light bulb on. Leave it on for ten minutes.
2. Hold the thermometer four inches from the side of the bulb. Wait one minute. Write down the temperature.
3. Hold the thermometer four inches below the bulb. Wait one minute. Write down the temperature.
4. Hold the thermometer four inches from the side of the bulb. Place a piece of cardboard

between the bulb and the thermometer. Wait one minute. Write down the temperature. It is lower because the rays will not pass through cardboard.

Observing the Decay of Molecules

You cannot handle radioactive materials. But in this experiment you can see one kind of decay process.

Materials:

- a small amount of luminescent, "glow-in-the-dark" paint (available at artists' supply stores)
- a 3" x 5" card
- a small paint brush

Procedure:

1. Brush some of the paint onto the card.
2. Hold the card in a bright light for one minute.
3. Take the card into a dark room. The paint will glow. Then the glow will slowly begin to fade.

The paint glows because light causes the paint molecules to become energized or "excited."

The glow fades and disappears because the molecules are losing their energy. They are decaying back to their "unexcited" or stable state. This process is very similar to the decay process in radioactive atoms.

There is an important difference between the paint molecules and radioactive atoms. When radioactive atoms decay, they change to nonradioactive atoms. The decay process ends when all the radioactive atoms are gone. In contrast, the paint molecules are not destroyed as they decay. They can be restored by again exposing them to a bright light.

Chronology

1867—Marie Sklowdoska is born in Warsaw, Poland (Russian Empire) on November 7.

1876—Sister, Zosia, dies.

1878—Mother dies.

1883—Graduates school.

1886—Marie becomes a governess.

1889—Moves back with her father.

1891—Enrolls at the Sorbonne.

1893—Earns her degree in physics

1894—Earns her degree in mathematics

1895—Marries Pierre Curie on July 26.

1897—Gives birth to her first child, Irene.

1898—Discovers two new elements, polonium and radium.

1903—Receives Ph.D. in physics on June 25.

Marie and Pierre receive the Nobel Prize for Physics jointly with Antoine Henri

Becquerel for their work in the field of radioactivity.

1904—Gives birth to second daughter, Eve.

1906—Pierre is killed by a horse-drawn wagon on April 19.

Marie takes over Pierre's professorship, and becomes the first woman to teach at the Sorbonne.

1911—Awarded a second Nobel Prize, this time for her work in chemistry.

1912—Becomes seriously ill, but later recovers.

1914—Paris Radium Institute opens, with Marie as director.

World War I begins.

1918—World War I ends.

Poland becomes an independent nation.

1921—Marie visits the United States and is presented with a gram of radium by President Warren G. Harding.

1926—Irene Curie marries Frederic Joliot.

1934—Marie Curie dies of leukemia, caused by exposure to radiation, July 4.

1935—Marie's daughter, Irene Joliot-Curie, and her husband, Frederic Joliot-Curie, are awarded the Nobel Prize in Chemistry for their discovery of artificial radioactivity.

Periodic Table of Elements

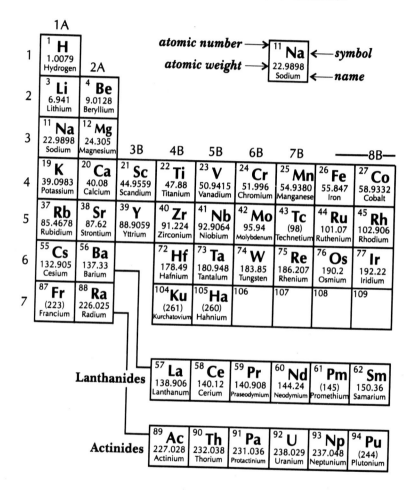

								8A
								2 **He** 4.00260 Helium
			3A	4A	5A	6A	7A	
			5 **B** 10.81 Boron	6 **C** 12.011 Carbon	7 **N** 14.0067 Nitrogen	8 **O** 15.9994 Oxygen	9 **F** 18.9984 Fluorine	10 **Ne** 20.179 Neon
—	1B	2B	13 **Al** 26.9815 Aluminum	14 **Si** 28.0855 Silicon	15 **P** 30.9738 Phosphorus	16 **S** 32.06 Sulfur	17 **Cl** 35.453 Chlorine	18 **Ar** 39.948 Argon
28 **Ni** 58.69 Nickel	29 **Cu** 63.546 Copper	30 **Zn** 65.39 Zinc	31 **Ga** 69.72 Gallium	32 **Ge** 72.59 Germanium	33 **As** 74.9216 Arsenic	34 **Se** 78.96 Selenium	35 **Br** 79.904 Bromine	36 **Kr** 83.80 Krypton
46 **Pd** 106.42 Palladium	47 **Ag** 107.868 Silver	48 **Cd** 112.41 Cadmium	49 **In** 114.82 Indium	50 **Sn** 118.71 Tin	51 **Sb** 121.75 Antimony	52 **Te** 127.60 Tellurium	53 **I** 126.905 Iodine	54 **Xe** 131.29 Xenon
78 **Pt** 195.08 Platinum	79 **Au** 196.967 Gold	80 **Hg** 200.59 Mercury	81 **Tl** 204.383 Thallium	82 **Pb** 207.2 Lead	83 **Bi** 208.980 Bismuth	84 **Po** (209) Polonium	85 **At** (210) Astatine	86 **Rn** (222) Radon

63 **Eu** 151.96 Europium	64 **Gd** 157.25 Gadolinium	65 **Tb** 158.925 Terbium	66 **Dy** 162.50 Dysprosium	67 **Ho** 164.930 Holmium	68 **Er** 167.26 Erbium	69 **Tm** 168.934 Thulium	70 **Yb** 173.04 Ytterbium	71 **Lu** 174.967 Lutetium

95 **Am** (243) Americium	96 **Cm** (247) Curium	97 **Bk** (247) Berkelium	98 **Cf** (251) Californium	99 **Es** (252) Einsteinium	100 **Fm** (257) Fermium	101 **Md** (258) Mendelevium	102 **No** (259) Nobelium	103 **Lr** (260) Lawrencium

Notes by Chapter

Chapter 1

1. Eve Curie, *Madame Curie* (Garden City, N.Y.: Doubleday, Doran & Co., 1937), p. 210.

2. Ibid., p. 220.

3. Rosalynd Pflaum, *Grand Obsession* (New York: Doubleday, 1989), p. 5.

4. Curie, p. 51.

5. Pflaum, p. 13.

Chapter 2

1. Curie, p. 57.

2. Pflaum, p. 18.

3. Curie, p. 80.

Chapter 3

1. Curie, p. 109.

2. Ibid., p. 119.

3. Ibid., p. 129.

Chapter 4

1. Curie, p. 161.

2. Ibid., p. 171.

3. Ibid., p. 177.

Chapter 5

1. Curie, p. 189.

2. Ibid., p. 191.

3. Ibid., p. 204.

Chapter 6

1. Curie, p. 217.

2. Ibid., p. 222.

3. Ibid., p. 242.

4. Ibid., p. 246.

5. Ibid., p. 259.

Chapter 7

1. Curie, p. 254.

2. Ibid., p. 252.

3. Ibid., p. 284.

Chapter 8

1. Curie, p. 287.

2. Ibid., p. 305.

Chapter 9

1. Pflaum, p. 235.

2. Curie, p. 324.

3. Ibid., p. 327.

4. Ibid., p. 347.

Chapter 10

1. Curie, p. 348.
2. Ibid., p. 366.
3. Ibid., p. 375.
4. Ibid., p. 375.

Chapter 11

1. Curie, p. 378.
2. Ibid., p. 381.
3. Ibid., p. 383

Glossary

active element—An element that gives off radiation.

atom—Tiny particles comprised of a nucleus and electrons that make up the various elements.

conductor—A substance or body that can transmit electricity or heat.

element—A substance that is made of only one kind of atom.

intensity—The measurement of radiation's strength.

ionize—To cause to become a conductor.

molecule—A group of atoms that are bonded together.

pitchblende—An ore that contains uranium and radium.

polonium—A radioactive element.

radiation—The process by which energy is given off by molecules and atoms.

radioactivity—The process of giving off rays.

radiology—The study of radioactive substances.

radium—A radioactive element.

uranium—A radioactive element.

X rays—Rays that can pass through various solid objects but not through bone.

Further Reading

Brandt, Keith. *Radioactivity*. Mahwah, N.J.: Troll, 1983.

Gleasner, Diana. *Breakthrough: Women in Science*. New York: Walker & Company, 1983.

Greene, Carol. *Poland*. Chicago: Children's Press, 1983.

Henry, Joanne. *Marie Curie*. New York: Macmillan, 1966.

McGowan, Tom. *Marie Curie*. New York: Watts, 1986.

McGowen, Tom. *World War I*. New York: Franklin Watts, 1993.

Milne, Lorus J. & Milne, Margery. *Understanding Radio-activity*. New York: Atheneum, 1989.

Rubin, Elizabeth. *The Curies and Radium*. New York: Watts, 1961.

Veglahn, Nancy. *The Mysterious Rays: Marie Curie's World*. New York: Coward, McCann, Geoghegan, 1977.

Internet Addresses

Centennial of the Discovery of Radioactivity
<http://www.ccr.jussieu.fr/radioactivite/english/
    accueil.htm>

Marie Curie and the Science of Radioactivity
<http://www.aip.org/history/curie/>

The Nobel Prize in Physics, 1903
<http://www.nobel.se/physics/laureates/1903/
    index.html>

The Nobel Prize in Chemistry, 1911
<http://www.nobel.se/chemistry/laureates/1911/
    index.html>

Polonium
<http://www.chemsoc.org/viselements/pages/data/
    polonium_data.html>

Radium
<http://www.chemsoc.org/viselements/pages/data/
    radium_data.html>

Index